What Do Grown-ups Do All Day?

by Virginie Morgand

WIDE EYED EDITIONS

Contents

Are you ready for an adventure?

Come with us and find out what grown-ups do...

What do grown-ups do all day?

On this trip we are going to visit 14 different workplaces, and in each place we are going to talk to eight people.

Each of the grown-ups you meet can be seen doing their job on the page before. Can you spot them all?

Every day, lots of grown-ups all around us head out the door, and we don't see them again until later that evening...

But what do they do all day?

Many people go to a special workplace to do a job. A job can mean all kinds of things – it can mean working inside a building or working outside in the fresh air.

Over time, people develop different kinds of skills and abilities to do their job better. They might become excellent at making things with their hands, or good at using certain kinds of machinery, or using their brain to come up with new ideas and solutions to problems.

Join us on our adventure as we visit some very different workplaces to see what kinds of jobs people do all day. Which one do you like best?

Welcome to our school

When you start school, you will be given a good education by your teachers – and this will help you do a job when you are a grown-up yourself! And while maths lessons and learning to read and write are important, at school you can also try art, drama and sports, too.

What do grown-ups do in a school?

I am the HEAD TEACHER. Welcome to our school!

I am a maths TEACHER

I run the school and make sure everyone feels happy and safe.

In my classroom you will learn to add and subtract... and lots more besides!

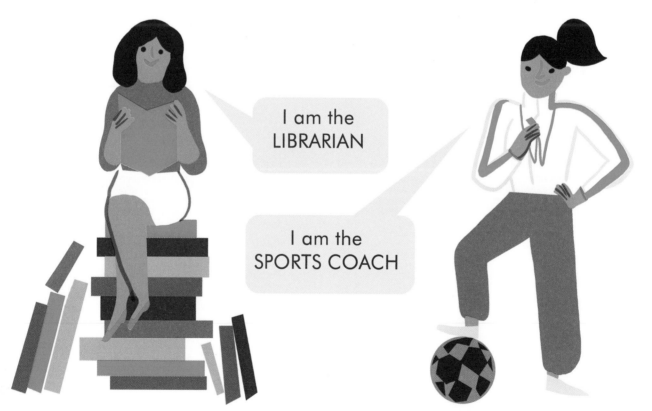

I am the LIBRARIAN

I am the SPORTS COACH

I look after the library and love to suggest good books for you to read.

I will play sports and games with you. Being active keeps you fit and healthy!

I am the DRAMA TEACHER

I am the CARETAKER

I will teach you how to act, and help to put on the school play every year.

I work hard to keep the school clean and tidy, and a safe place for children.

I am the MUSIC TEACHER

I am a STUDENT

Come and sing in my choir, or learn an instrument with me.

I'm not a grown-up... yet! I go to school every day with my friends.

Welcome to the hospital

If you are poorly, you might go to a hospital. Here, doctors and nurses work together to find out what is making you unwell, and try to put it right, whether it be by fixing a broken bone or giving you medicine to make you feel better. But a hospital isn't just a place for sick patients – new babies are born here too.

EMERGENCY

What do grown-ups do in a hospital?

I try to find out what is making a patient ill, and help them feel better.

I look after sick patients day and night, and give them their medicine.

I help patients recover through movement and special exercises.

I prepare medication that will help patients feel better and overcome illness.

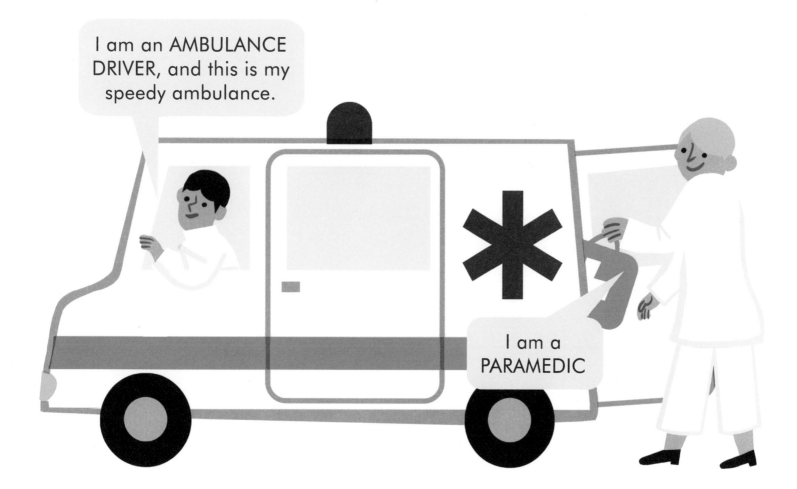

In an emergency, I drive the ambulance that will take a patient to hospital.

I travel in the ambulance and give first aid to anyone who needs it.

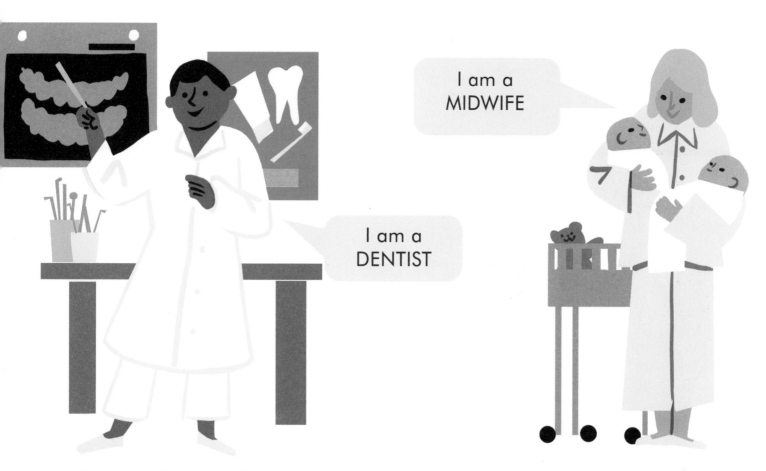

I take care of your teeth and gums – don't forget to floss at night!

I help deliver children into the world, and look after the newborn babies.

Welcome to the farm

Have you ever wondered where the food on your plate comes from? Nearly everything you eat – meat, vegetables and even grain for your bread – was grown or reared by a farmer. A lot of care goes into looking after everything on a farm. Just take a look!

What do grown-ups do on a farm?

I am a FARMER

I DRIVE the TRACTOR

I grow crops and raise animals to make the food that is on your plate!

With my tractor, I plough the fields, sow seeds and harvest the crops.

I am a SHEPHERD

I am the MECHANIC

I tend to the farm's flock of sheep. My sheepdog helps me to round them up!

I look after the machinery on the farm, and fix the tractor if it goes wrong.

I am an animal doctor and make sure that the farm animals are healthy.

The milk that comes from cows also makes yoghurt and cheese!

I do all kinds of jobs to help the farmer, like feeding the animals.

I grow all kinds of fruits and vegetables, and keep the gardens looking pretty.

Welcome to the construction site

Whether you live in a small, historic village or a busy, modern city, everything around you was once built by skilled workers. As a building goes up, the area around it is called a construction site. If you visit one, hold onto your hard hat and look out for dangerous machines and heavy objects.

What do grown-ups do on a construction site?

I plan and design buildings before they are constructed.

Using my expert knowledge, I make sure that buildings won't fall down!

I put wires in the building, which provide you with electrical power and light.

I fix the pipes so that you have running water.

I am strong and carry heavy loads, dig the ground – and demolish things!

Buildings look much nicer once I've covered them with paint!

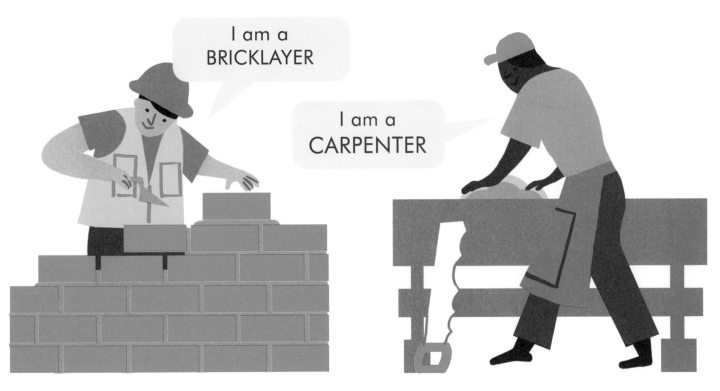

By putting up walls and tiling the roof, I make a building warm and dry.

I am especially good at making things out of wood.

Welcome to the shops

The shops are always full of hustle and bustle! Busy shoppers wander up and down the high street – and the shopkeepers who work here keep their stores stocked full of the things that people have come here to buy!

greens

BAKERY

MEATS

flowers

↑SHOP

BOOKS

23

What do grown-ups do at the shops?

I am a BUTCHER

I am a BAKER

I have a shop where I sell meat to my customers, who take it home to cook.

My bakery is full of the delicious breads and cakes that I have baked.

I am a GREENGROCER

I am a FLORIST

I sell all kinds of juicy fruits and ripe vegetables from my stall.

I make up beautiful bouquets of flowers for people, which I sell from my stall.

I have shelves full of books in my shop, and I can find the right one for everyone!

Come to my salon and I will make you feel special with a new haircut.

As you wander through the shop, I make sure you can find what you need.

I am out for a busy day of shopping – I have lots of things on my list to buy!

Welcome to the theatre

Going to the theatre is a real treat! The actors there will make you laugh, cry and sit on the edge of your seat as the drama unfolds. But putting on a performance takes a whole team of people behind the scenes too, who create costumes, scenery, sound effects and lighting, to transport you to another world.

What do grown-ups do in the theatre?

I am an
ACTOR

I am a
DIRECTOR

I act the part of a character in a play...
and I have lots of lines to remember!

I give instructions to the actors during rehearsals,
to make sure the play turns out well.

I am a
MAKE UP
ARTIST

I am a SET
DESIGNER

I help the actors transform themselves to
play their part by putting their make up on.

I design the stage to show the
audience where the play is set.

The clothes that actors wear on stage are called costumes – and I have designed them all!

This play was written by me! I imagined all the characters and their storylines.

In the dark pauses between scenes, I move the set around the stage.

The theatre can be dark, so I show people to their seats with my little torch.

Welcome to the action!

Some jobs are full of adventure and can be dangerous, too. Often, the people who do them bravely put their own safety on the line to help others. They must stay fit and train for a long time to have the skills they need to stay safe. Many of these jobs used to be done by men only, but now lots of women do them too, and they are just as good at them!

31

Who has an action-packed job?

I am in the army. I travel around the world in service of my country, to keep the peace.

I am in the navy. Instead of being on land, I defend my country by travelling the seas.

I am the pilot of this helicopter. Helicopters don't need a runway, like planes – they can take off straight from the ground.

I have a secret mission, which I can't tell you about! I keep an eye on things and investigate to discover information.

I travel into space in my rocket! My mission is to explore our solar system to understand it better.

I investigate crimes and arrest criminals if they break the law.

When I hear there is a fire, I jump in my fire engine and race to the scene to put the fire out with my water hose.

I am a bit of a daredevil! I stand in for an actor and perform dangerous stunts in a film, like crashes, jumps or fights.

Welcome to the hotel

If you are travelling to a new part of the world, you might stay in a hotel while you are there. Hotels can be huge – with space for hundreds of people – or just have a few rooms, but either way, everyone there will be working hard to make sure you eat well and have a good night's sleep before you go out to explore the next day. Bon voyage!

What do grown-ups do in a hotel?

I am the HOTEL MANAGER

I am in charge of the hotel and I oversee all the people that work here.

I am the RECEPTIONIST

I greet guests when they arrive at our hotel and help with their questions.

I am the PORTER

Some people call me the bellboy. I am here to help you with your bags!

I am the CONCIERGE

If you want to book tickets for a trip, ask me to make a reservation for you.

While you are out for the day, I make sure your room is clean and tidy.

Breakfast, lunch and dinner – I cook them all for hundreds of guests every day!

I take your order and serve you your food at the restaurant. Bon Appétit!

I am staying at the hotel on my visit away from home.

Welcome to the great outdoors!

You have to work indoors for lots of jobs... but not for all of them! Whether you prefer spending time at the beach, at the park, in the mountains or even underwater, there's a job for you!

What do grown-ups do outdoors?

I look out to sea to check that everyone's safe, and if someone is in trouble, I rescue them!

I sit on the waterfront with my rod to catch fish and sell them to be eaten.

I teach people how to have fun in the water, surfing or windsurfing.

I study the wildlife in the sea, from the tiniest plankton to the biggest whale!

I look after the park and the wildlife here, and I also give guided tours!

I make sure the trees are safe, and saw off any dangerous branches.

I work to protect animals and the environment, and teach people about them.

I help people have fun outdoors – safely! – climbing and mountaineering.

Welcome to the concert hall

Some people are amazing singers, others can play a musical instrument – and if you want to see them perform, you can head to the lavish surroundings of the concert hall.

What do grown-ups do in the concert hall?

I show the orchestra how slow (or fast!) and how quiet (or loud!) they should play.

I play a musical instrument and perform with the rest of the orchestra.

My work is to sing with my beautiful voice. Sometimes a choir joins in, too.

I have written the music being played at this concert house!

I am the photographer, here to take pictures of the musicians playing.

If you want to watch a performance, you can buy a ticket from me!

I control the lights in the concert hall, which can make the performance more dramatic.

I am here to enjoy the show and listen to the wonderful music!

Welcome to the newsroom

Every day, the news is broadcast on televisions to tell us about the important events happening around the world. On screen, you might only see one or two presenters, but it takes a big team of people to investigate the facts and film the show. Take a look and see for yourself.

What do grown-ups do in the newsroom?

I report the news – and I often help to research the facts and write the stories beforehand, too.

I am a journalist. I investigate stories and interview people.

I work for the government, and I'm here to talk about what I have been doing.

I gather scientific information to predict the weather for the week ahead.

When we broadcast the news, I am behind the scenes, filming.

I gather the research together and decide what should be on the news that day.

I lead the film crew and am in control of everything as the programme broadcasts.

I update the website and put news stories online.

Welcome to the gym

You might have noticed that a lot of jobs involve sitting down for long parts of the day... and that isn't good for staying fit and healthy! Because of this, lots of grown-ups head to the gym, to do classes and get active to make sure they stay in good shape.

What do grown-ups do in the gym?

I work out in the gym and help people improve their fitness.

I give energetic dance classes – dancing is a fun way to keep active!

I show people the right way to stretch and move into different yoga positions.

I work one-to-one with people, encouraging them as they exercise.

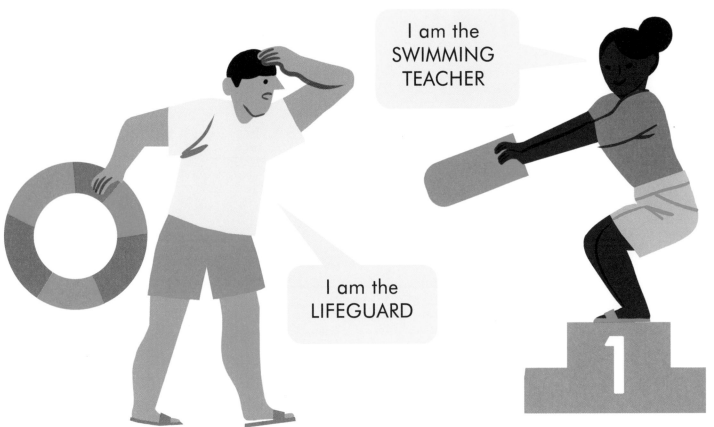

I keep watch by the pool and check that everyone in the water stays safe.

I teach people how to stay afloat in the water and become good swimmers.

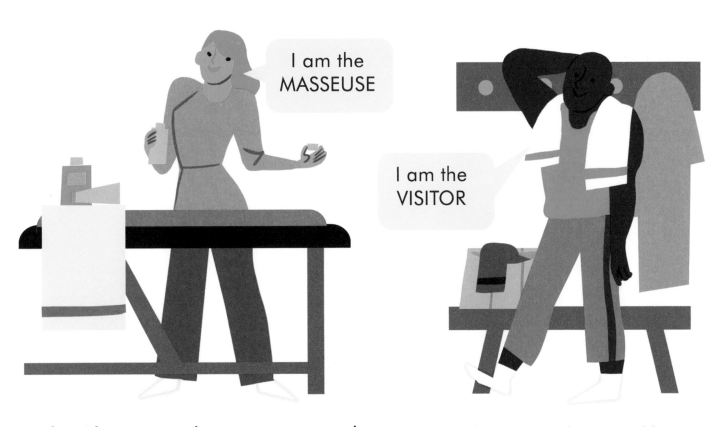

People with sore muscles come to me and I soothe their pain with massage.

I come here to work out and keep my body fit. Exercising makes me feel good!

Welcome to the university

Many of the jobs in this book need the person doing it to understand and use difficult information, which goes beyond what they might have learned at school.

Universities are a place where grown-ups go to get this extra education from clever professors, who have studied their specific subject for years and years. You can study all kinds of things – take a look!

55

What do grown-ups do at the university?

I make sure all the different departments are running smoothly.

I keep everyone who works here organised and in touch with each other.

I research chemicals and materials, and help my students to study them, too.

I study animals and wildlife and give lectures to my students about them.

I think space is fascinating and use my research to explore new theories about it.

I am interested literature, art and music, and teach my students about them.

I have been invited here to make art and inspire the students with my creativity.

I come to the university to learn, and will leave when I have completed my degree.

Welcome to the airport

Everyone who has a job takes a holiday now and then – often overseas! In the old days, going to another country meant travelling across land and sea, and often took days, weeks, or even months!

Today, we can just hop on a plane and fly thousands of miles in a matter of hours. You leave – and arrive – from an airport, and the people there work hard to make sure your trip is comfortable, and most of all, safe.

What do grown-ups do at the airport?

I am in charge of everyone on the plane, and will safely fly you to your destination.

I am here to support the captain and help to fly the plane when he takes a break.

Passenger safety is my number one priority as I look after you on board this plane.

I enjoy physical work! My job is to load and unload the passengers' luggage from the planes between flights.

I book customers onto their flights and send their luggage to be loaded onto the right plane.

I check everyone's passport so that we know who is leaving and who is arriving in the country.

I keep track of all the planes, making sure each one has enough space in the sky.

My dog is specially trained to sniff out things that people aren't supposed to bring into the country.

Index

First published in Great Britain in 2016 by Wide Eyed Editions,
an imprint of Aurum Press, 74–77 White Lion Street, London N1 9PF
QuartoKnows.com
Visit our blogs at QuartoKnows.com

A catalogue record for this book is available from the British Library.

ISBN 978-1-84780-809-7

The illustrations were created digitally
Set in Futura

Designed by Andrew Watson
Edited by Jenny Broom
Published by Rachel Williams

Printed in China

3 5 7 9 8 6 4 2